Living with Time

Living with Time

Poems by

Libby VanBuskirk

Cover design by Shay Culligan
Cover image: "Reflections" by David Conrad

ISBN: 979-8-90146-601-8
Library of Congress Control Number: 2026931890

Kelsay Books
502 South 1040 East, A-119
American Fork, Utah 84003
Kelsaybooks.com

With gratitude for my wonderful family,
especially Katharine, Coeli, Eric, Van Anh, Lisa,
Margot, Susan, Sally, Dave, Bill, and Betty
and for my late husband, Dave,
and the many projects we shared.

Acknowledgments

With special appreciation to my friend and fellow poet, Jeanne Svensson who served as editor from the beginning of the book, my inspiring poetry teachers Rebecca Starks and David Weinstock, members of The Otter Creek Poets and The Line Tamers, Matilda Stoddard, my astute readers David Conrad and Bill Stephany; with gratitude to Robert Pierattini and Julian Sprague. Finally, with appreciation to the editors of the publications where the following poems have appeared:

Abrazos Anthology: "Dry September"
Adison Independent, Middlebury, Vermont: "Inside the Mists of Morning"
The Aurorean: "Listening to Faure's Requiem on a Saturday Morning in May"
Beloit Poetry Journal: "Dry September"
Birchsong Anthology: "Listening to Faure's Requiem on a Saturday Morning in May"
Blueline: "Wild Lake"
Cold Lake Anthology: "Children of Midnight," "Where We Found Spring"
Maps and Voyages Anthology: "Front and Back, Dark and Light"
Neologism Poetry Journal: "Kindling"
The Orchard Poetry Journal: "On a Bright Winter Day," "Living with Time"
Passager Journal: "Closing for Winter"
Quartet: "Invisible"
Rutland Herald, Vermont: "Inside the Mists of Morning"
San Pedro River Review: "Touchsounds"
Vermont Voices Anthology: "Still Life"
WayWords Literary Journal: "The Nightmare Theater"
Zig Zag Lit Magazine Anthology: "Huckleberry Woman"

Contents

TWO

THREE

ONE

Another Bright Winter Day

Another winter day so long ago
we five skated in the cove
where the river in its myth and mystery
turned and returned, its puzzling course
tricking my inner compass,
opening surprising country views
so near the city. We could skate close
or, easier for the teenagers, far apart.

Houses steep above suggested
some small town in Switzerland
like those under our Christmas tree,
calm in white perfection, a real village
where families shovel snow in piles off ice
for those like us
to winter-skate in smooth togetherness.
Our blades woke tiny windstorms.
We moved with speed and grace like low birds
following the frozen river's eccentric course
beside shores of leaning pines
or under open sky with white cloud streamers
drifting in and out of otherwise perfect blue
on this day, the last or almost last our family
would choose an outing at the same time and place.

I wrote with gigantic cursive strokes
on the brilliant white page beneath my feet,
seeing something resembling beauty everywhere,
even in the particles of cast-back cut-up ice;

a day where the lyric could live, the “I” or “we” of possibility,
when the youngest could still remain within sight,
the children’s father and I
could still skate holding hands
and winter could still freeze a river
to safely hold us all,
the ice so solid, so deep.

Listening to Faure's Requiem on a Saturday Morning in May

When it's my time, let me not miss
springtime in Vermont. Windows open,
thrushes, warblers, chickadees,
spangled flute songs,
and on the radio children's voices
in an old cathedral bringing *Requiem aeternam.*

Melted I am from the white void
by the alchemy that transforms twigs and buds
to baby greens and full-leafed trees
open to the eye of the sky.
Yellow daffodils, lately entombed,
rise to multiply on the meadow slope.

Robin couples flutter, nesting
near peach and purple tulips.
Spring lets its fledglings loose.
I move my arms, conducting orchestra
and chorus, directing last snow
everywhere else to also melt.

We've been together for so long,
the world and I.
Kyrie eleison. How I wish to hold in mind
Mount Philo and the mountains that enclose us,
our love alive in the family of Vermont springtime,
Greek phrases of grace.
Kyrie eleison, lord have mercy,
coming in the clear voices of children.

Where We Found Spring

We paddled near the past event,
the fallen maple
long in length, lying in lake water,
trunk severed and bent,
orange insides stripped and spilling,
but still blooming
baby green spring leaves.

Only the mountains lately witnessed
the ferocity. But today we were part
of our own occasion—he with his camera,
I with notebook and pen.

We longed to pull close, touch
the forsaken tree, but paused
before a spread-out thin pollen island
attached to the fallen tree
like a cobweb excessively anchored.

We could not be the knife
to cut the golden floating cover,
no solid weaving but the thinnest cloth
of unconnected dots, fresh-fallen,
amply clustered on the cold and quiet lake.
We paused beside this delicate tribute to spring
which sometime soon
would surely wobble out of our shared time.

To the Lake

I will arise and go now, and go to Innisfree
—W. B. Yeats

No bee-loud glade, nor shelter made with wattles,
but weathered cedar—our distant dwelling, patched, rebalanced,
hoisted up and resting on sand, the spit of land, surrounded
by erratic lake and stream. Early we come each year,
to elevate our senses.

Sometimes the beach goes under. House steps lead
to shallow water. Or the grove beside my far-side study
may receive small water offerings until I meditate beside
a pond of ferns and submerged wildflowers. Such is our retreat,
this peninsula, a north country lake.

We live low, the lake rises and falls.
We welcome change perpetual, attuning soul and spirit to raw life,
monstrous winds that make me cower—
Will such force expand to peril?
When pressure inside mounts, dare I crack a window?

Easy days on the shaded porch, our hallowed lookout
near sand and water, spiders on shabby screens,
I glide into the old metal armchair that bends with weight.
Beyond my open notebook, I half expect deer, bear or moose
to crash through trees and stand before us.

Later, when family members gather, several
who see each other only once a year, we swim lengths or sail,
climb mountains, hefting our dogs through narrow channels,
dine outside in candled darkness, charged by love—
until summer ends, lake time wanes and close ones leave by relay.

We pack up for the season, lock doors, drive to our winter life.
But even through the cold months, before sleep,
my mind calls forth outside my window
the sound of easy waves, moving forward
and gently moving back.

Living with Time

Once when time's long waves swallowed the soft-sand beach
I could hardly feel momentum wash beneath my feet.
Though it seized a small piece of me before it slipped back,
I remained nearly the same, but for that scant touch.

Soon I found Time in our grandmother clock, always in the hall,
elegant but remote. I watched her thin pointed fingers
keeping hours in her polished case. Never relaxed, her hands
tried each moment, then moved on—how fast she ran distances.

But time did not chime warnings to save me from lateness.
No rooster, mornings she never stops to waken me,
nor will she shush me to sleep at night. *Three AM! Not again!*
When I lose Time, trouble finds me. But no help can I expect.

Time, you've allotted my full share of years, for free.
But I foresee abandonment, you racing on, oblivious, without me.

Testing Bowley Brook

Spring again
and up the mystery course
my journey each year to assess
the long winter's revision.
I raise my paddle   twist the blue canoe
between sand spits and flotsam.

Last Autumn
the brook ran thin as a string
water drawn to clouds
after long days of summer heat.

Today   deep passage.
I paddle above underwater ripples
of sun-lit sand   a drenched desert.
Sweet clarity   if I'd brought a cup
I could sip the taste of mountains.

On one side
loosened roots corkscrew down
from dislodged dirt. Lightly rooted trees
bend   a tangled archway overhead.
A quick grab   I hold back handfuls
of branches   bend low and
thrust the canoe under the thicket.

A daisy meadow opens up
my spirit christened by abundant white
under untouched blue sky.

Toward a turn

and the current strengthens.
May the God of this Brook
allow me as far as I can go—
Let me find the waterfall.

In response   nipping waves
challenge the canoe. The brook spreads,
a miniature pond, its surface sparkling.
I hear the waterfalls' cascade.
I feel droplets   wet breeze.

A quick glimpse   rising spray
shards of rainbow   and
a force stronger than any I've known
spins me around   splats me over waves
sends me away.

Bow high   I do not topple
but repositioned   paddle on lap
hurtle down-stream   returning
to my source
the lake calling me home.

Inside the Mists of Morning

Late spring.
Ducks vee into nearby reeds,
rustling toward flight

while elsewhere morning scrim slowly
rises from the lake,
loosening peepholes along the shoreline.

Pinpricks of light sample familiar mountains
and stone-outcroppings,
bits of pale water.

Lopey ghosts,
those soft and racing sky-spirits,
skim above the steaming lake field.

On the lake's far side, jagged trees
that jut in and out along peninsulas and coves
have not yet appeared

but what is stored in the known will awaken.

The Pump

To lie here by the lake,
away from cars and horns,
blasts of alert,
a blotter of smells,
to lie
between mended sheets,
to stay with the silent moon
and falling stars,
to use my share,
nothing more.

But all night the pump
runs and sucks, a mindless device
gone berserk, calling for more,
gulping the lake to refill
our man-high pressure tank.

Maybe by morning I'll find a helper
to travel the miles, to answer my call.
I try to sleep to the cackles and burps,
scratches and slurps, as water pulled in
seeps out, somewhere in the darkness.

Half asleep I dream
that no one can find what can never end,
the pumping, stopping, running, sucking—
distress, even here, how can it be met?

A machine set in motion
that stretches so far
its intake must snap at the feet of the loons.
Though dreams may hold me tight,
I cannot miss their calls.

On a Night Like This

Whatever strolls outside I cannot hear, this night so still
not even wind chimes or calls of distant loons linger
to echo in our midnight dreams. Far away—the swelter
of today's picnic, when tall trees brought welcome shade,
predicting cool dark hours like these. Praise
the serene and silent moon that slips below the mountain.
Stars rest in peace their cool brilliance. May such nights,
as in past summers, long sustain tonight's contentment.

Far out, the anchored sailboat's bow will turn. These days wind
blows hurricanes or fierce remainders after flooding bayous,
our new weather. Gales can send water funnels strutting
across the lake, approaching like other world invaders.

If such surges topple giant pines, will we crowd for safety
beneath the stairs? May disaster never overcome our haven.

Porch Talk by the Lake

Candlelight
bends with our breathing.
With dinner long done, the young in bed,
we talk of the year, anxious to share
their tales of wolves, their spooks,
their changing moods. Mice seen walking in boots,
breadcrumbs laid, deadly mushrooms,
the little dig to China.
Who can make a dog talk?
How long till we go to the lake? Stars so bright.
Science, alchemy, astronomy.

We stay in the nearly dark, recounting events,
puttering with words,
naming what we have seen and what we may never see.

On the lake, a few red lights,
slow boats
paused in alternate time and open space.

The forest of pine
breathes silence, a softness between us.
The children are safe in their bunks,
hidden upstairs from our fears—our wolves
overgrown, the surging packs,
the rising seas, bombs and burning.

By water, mountains, sand and trees,
let enchantment hold them safe,

from all we know
and their time ahead.

We murmur into the fresh air,
our words only as loud
as the low back-hum of peepers
mating outside in the darkness.

Swimming

For Eric at Twelve

When you push off
you will swim leagues
I have not known,
into log jams unthinkable,
waterways yet unfounded,

not just across this lake,
a boat bumping
at your heels, the loons' arpeggio
in the distance leaving you
their recent pass.

Your days may prove unclear, no sun
to warm the stretching fingers
that knead you into motion.
You will find knowledge
of underwater schools,
from more than fishing.
Seaweed sways sudden nets
testing the legs of crawlers.

Curiosity will float your pulling
as you wrinkle in waves,
your brain straining toward the sea.
Fine line drawings you leave behind
will wash out onto the millpond.

Where Are We?

For Katharine

Uphill, on that rough old road,
we headed toward a cool fern-floor forest
and high meadow
lush with wild strawberries and buttercups,
eager to sink the red Guatemalan cloth
in tall grass and lay out our treats.

I picked a wild flower bouquet
as we followed the others,
our kids, their cousins,
aunts and uncles and our dog,
all swinging coolers, baskets and packs,
talking in the language of memories.

Breathing the welcome scent of pine,
my lungs awakened with glory.
Like little ones in a tale, we quickened our pace
as if beckoned, following the scent,
pine pine pine, stronger than ever.

The kids ahead called, *Where are we?*
Must be the wrong road!
We hurried toward them,
soon stumbling into deep tire tracks,
tripping on ripped branches and strewn pinecones.

Nothing familiar. No trees
but a cemetery of stumps.

An upturned place, every stem slashed,
a graveyard of sticks, holes and hollows,
death in thousands of stems,
roots and leaves.

Bulldozed beyond our reach,
old paths hung in pieces.
Chunks dangled like lifeless bodies,
uprooted memories.
A whole forest gone, rejected pieces underfoot.
Dust wrapped each ripped fern.

On a piece of birch bark
our son scribbled a note
and hid it under a familiar border.

We laid on fresh pine boughs.

Light Lake Night

White crescent light,
the great dipper
cups the sky's fluid,
pours from the milky way
into the long wide lake
its milky likeness.

Deep night
the lake settles,
a melting ice floe
with stars embedded
in spring
already seeming summer.
A milky stare,
a cow's soft eye.
Light lake night.

Morning

After days of rain
sun spots spin to life
on every tree.

Blue
expands in the sky
until sky flocks float
on a blue lake.

My mind's night bubble pops.
Oh, fragile dawn, you grew
before you woke me.

Old Birch by the Forest Path

This old birch
attracts the finest light.
From its sides
pages peel away
in hieroglyphic particularity.
Woodpeckers' old codes.
expand to giant typeface.

Long scrolls wind
against the base and curl back
where their deep waves
break open from inside
revealing the legends of growth.

Here early explorers
long ago crept in
and through hidden tunnels
brought their treasures out.

Higher up
beside the tree's thick trunk
six small beaks open wide
while below,
exposed by fresh new peels,
scant virgin skin
develops in the sun.

Still Life After the Arrangement

Wildflower remains
          lie tangled on the cutting board.
No longer color-clustered as in their zones in the fields.
                    A few whole daisies
           orange paintbrushes   alive and open by day
still show small flames
                              closing in the discard pile.
The clover   picked-over for this selection
                    bring green and purple to the heap.
A bee would want this surfeit.

Small disassembled
          buttercup wings
                    waterproof and bright
and the shrunken buds   like bugs   brown and drying
                    I sweep
into sweet confetti
          along with the every-which-way
of pickup-stick stems.
                    Plenty remains for the compost heap.
But first

Come, My Love. And bring your camera.

Great Blue Heron

With halted bridesmaid steps
you wade
through lights of water
rustling lengths of shallow water grass.

Where currents scarcely stir
beside you in the bay
you stay.
Maybe you feel a snail move,
a crawler sigh,
minnows pass.
Maybe you're sensing
clouds that stir the sky
or moss trails
on a stone face.

I move
toward you
from the shade.
Filaments that hold you snap.
You flap
and lift above the water,
over driftwood trees
descend,
and beside another crescent beach
begin again
your still silence.

Touch Sounds

Off season. November night wind
hurtled through the mountain pass,
howled across the lake.
Dark outside met dark inside.

Mattress, blankets,
pillows, quilt,
the hearth ablaze.
We settled beside the blooming fire
wrapped together,
bodies calmed for listening.

With high-pitched creaks
wind pushed through every chink.
Nails stretched their pinnings.
Branches typed on sky lights,
wind knocked on doors.

Outside
the fox, the bobcat,
forced to find retreat.
Trees flung branches and bowed.
Inside
we roamed each other's territories.
Cold without and warm within.

Painted Nights

Some nights we walked to town
as if in blindness,
trusting memories
to keep us on the right-of-way.

We were unwilling
to interrupt the night with light
or alter a surprise that might emerge
from darkness.

But on some nights, we brought flashlights.
Our beams could obliterate
the Milky Way, blot out the northern sky,
every star.

With Jackson Pollock zeal
we pointed through openings in branches,
swirling flashlight-dots, blotches, streamers
into the nearby woods.

With brushes of light
we made still-life compositions,
assembling asters, goldenrod,
infant pines, tall grasses, new scat.

In chiaroscuro we scribbled each other,
temporary portraits.
We added finds we never saw by day,
elements of movement, changing time.

Little History

I grew up
but never left
I walked and ran
toward the far world
but not
far enough to not
look back
        we always do return

I found space on the old ceiling
to walk
and I walked
        high above the years
my feet sticky from plum jelly
spilled before I leapt

my tracks
were not too sticky
to stop me

I left no marks

Our War

If
we had known
that daring missions occurred far away,
that war would never come
to our own Pennsylvania,
if we had not chosen
the downtown movie theater
as conduit for true views
of the world and war—
where we saw glamorous Veronica fall,
flirting with Nazi officers to let her buddies escape,
and watched pretty French girls
run through underbrush,
pointing flashlights
to conjure friendly parachutists from the black sky,

if
Grandad had not told hushed tales
of night watches atop nearby buildings
scouting for any errant enemy plane, or Dad
had not brought home samples from the plant,
saying *Every rivet must be perfect,*
we can't lose our brave boys,

then,
when visiting my country friend,
in those Autumn days of 1943
we two girls might not have run
far into the woods,

on the lookout for danger,
seeking hidden hide-outs and enemy invaders,
straining to create our own heroic scenes
of clever rescue and escape.

If
when we came upon
the little cottage in the wood
I had not tried the knob,
my friend not helped
the door creep open,

then
we would not have stepped into the beam
of charged white light
sent from a high window. Sparkling
particles floated our whole selves
onto a ready-made stage.
Bright colors moved out of darkness
while every dim presence
served as an audience,
sending silent encouragement.

We took no time to look around.
Our hands reached high and low,
grabbing crucial objects
surely needed for our survival,
dropping the loot into red table napkins.

If
I had not called *Run!*
we might not have retreated so fast.

How we ran with our seized weapons—
perfume atomizers—held before us
as we moved forward.
Would either dare spray the fatal potion
into a sudden enemy's eyes,
even to save our own lives?

We stumbled through the woods,
hearing pursuers crunching branches
behind us on the path,
we tripped on an up-slung root
and both came down, knees first.

If
the forest floor had not risen up
to fill our bloody cuts
with pebbles, particles of dirt,
if our pride had not been sealed
with scars to last forever,
proof of encounter

then
we might not have bent under an old beech
to dig a hole. How speedily we threw in
the shiny spoons, candies,

matching red toothbrushes,
comb, canned Spam, fish lures, all.
I briefly wondered which might be real,
existing in the every-day of our familiar world,
and which unreal, known only to those
who lived and battled, so far from us.

We scattered dirt into our pit,
covered the disturbance
with leaves, and murmured incantations.

If
we hadn't realized this would be our only mission,
then
we would not have willed the day's exploit
to remain secret forever.

We seldom saw each other.
I heard nothing of the secluded cottage.
We never spoke again of our war
in the mountain woods of Pennsylvania.

Strolling at Dusk

In the east meadow orange paintbrushes close
for the night. Daisies seem spreading
but have already peaked. Wild flowers incline
toward the margin of late light and butterflies
that earlier hung and suckled
on every bloom have left.

Our dog nearby runs back and forth, checking
the road, our right-of-way, sniffing
with apparent glee. The meadow feels unfamiliar
early in the season, original in late light.
I pass the farmhouse, cultivator disks
and rusted baling gear down by the barn.
I'll need a scythe to lower our tall grass
before my husband comes tomorrow.

By the fence I picture our son. At twelve
he was an easy pasture-walker, casual
with grazing bulls, raising rusty barbs
like holy sparks to joyfully cut across.
The spring the green fields flooded,
he claimed the risen water an extra lake,
deriving a name from his name and a friend's.
In the overflowing steam
the two boys rode brilliant yellow rafts
as I stood by the bank, powerful in my terror.

Now he lives across an ocean,
beyond sight. I walk by the meadow, staying
on the road the way parents do. The fields are full,
and this is the warm dry night needed before haying.

Rocksound Point

Small stones like ball-bearings
roll me high
above the sea   salt air of sea
this miniature peninsula made
wholly of stones
I name
Rocksound Point.

No umbrella steadies me
but arms flung out
I glide
over speckled blue stones   sun-lit agates
wish stones   jewels of mica
orphans broken by time
centuries of stone   their slight
shifting
soft rolling anthems
playing on the welcome
of my ears
like a homecoming.

Avid collector   today
I pass   without taking.

A Summer Night

She brought the moon. He brought stars.
She brought a loaf of bread. He, wine.
They sat on the dock
and what they brought to taste
tasted like the night.

A soft night.
They trailed their feet in the warm water
until, too hot for clothes
they hastily undressed
falling back together
on the dock's weathered planks.

She let go and the moon
splashed beside the hitched canoe.
He released the stars
to sparkle in the water
where the frogs finally shushed.

They slept
and woke and slept again
all that sweet summer night.

Woman Feeding Seagulls

It takes little to lift them.
On the wharf   the slightest sprinkling of crumbs
    sifts through her cart
and heads pop up   poke down
wings interspersing.

She strains in her tight and skimpy coat
working to rip the sack saved for her
at the bakery.

From the whole world they come
birds beneath her raised arms
birds surrounding her lace-less shoes
    straddling moorings   skittering over ladders
strutting beside nets
ropes   dock pilings.

Her sleeve tightens
as she shakes out the last crumbs,
        All gone   my flyers
        All gone dear ones   darlings
the birds rise
shadows overlapping on the rough boards.

She watches their leave-taking
and, with small contented smiles, turns,
to clank her cart back onto asphalt.

Action Painting

Her brush strokes
must reach high
to make the first wave shatter.
Ocean blue turns
to tinsel light.

With white swirls
she over-paints,
brush
flashing,
over-splashing.

Too much blue ocean
Each fall
overcomes all.
Blue wave blue wave
blue wave,

all
slide
over
what blue must overtake
for more space.

Waves soon
rush far
beyond shore,
each fall sliding,
over sand, over land.

She stick-paints
children on the beach
jumping up from play,
mother stumbling,
baby crying.

Waves waves
high water over past-land,
white foam
follows,
paintbrush loaded.

On and on, blue and white
ocean spreading,
stretching
toward all edges
of the canvas.

The Shape Under the Dock

In
shallows
under the dock
the tiger's stripes quiver.

Thin lines
between dock slats
pattern its waiting self.

Small waves
shake the shadow's shape until
words rise—

> *Stay put. Stay put.*
> *Nowhere to go today.*
> *No gale winds or thunder.*
> *Sooth your souls.*
> *Collect pebbles and shells.*
> *Build castles of sand.*

Dry September

9/11/2002, the Year After

It has been not raining
all day; drought refuses forecast.
Maples by the road rattle paper leaves
and ferns fade my memory of green,
turning to skeleton
gauze undercover.

We live by a tide-out lake.
When at dawn the moose come to drink,
spots of land arise
like raised footprints of ancients.
When the wind blows,
waves move toward shore
not like water,
breaking in glory,
but sand-sifted, sand,
thirsty for sand.

I drink a cup of water
from a still-giving well,
weep dry
for the tallest pines and old white birch.
Our leader tells us
we must pour out the water
from our shoes. We must buy
gasoline; we must brush our teeth.
We must understand
that we do not understand.
We must go to war.

Wild Fire Lake

The lake floats skyscraper-tall blazes
before the slightest winds collapse
scarlet walls and flaming windows.
Tonight's entire lake surface, wild fire?

Water striders incite wide circles
expanding like breeze-carried sparks
that skim above the dark deep below,
where, in sanctuary pass catfish, pike, bass.

Onshore, shadows, unable to stand straight—
like their originals, lean against dark pines
in the sunset's last conflagration.
Stiff shore-born twigs reach as if searching for night dens.

Dark lake, blue-black mountains. That's all.
The sun's vast fire so quickly self-extinguished.

Closing for Winter

We've put the place to bed for winter.
All this rain, both lake and brook
keep coming up in all the low places.
We hauled each puddle to the dump.
Every poplar, spruce and pine, we hid
from the beavers. Into the woods we took
everything that calls for *Watch out!*
Don't step there. Next spring
we'll set the whole lot out again.
Same with the ferns and low-clumped moss.

The sun's already put away.
So are the mountains that floated
on the lake these past months.
The trim's left-over semi-gloss
we used to paint out the waves.

We caulked between logs,
took down views from every window.
After we got each opening shuttered,
all but the sky lights—too high—
we wrapped the candles on the mantel
in black plastic. From a little distance
you'd think they're waiting bats.
Inside it's dark as a mole hole at night,
fireplace stones cold as a toad's back.

We've just pulled down the stars.
That was the hardest.

Wild Lake

I will miss your repertoire of gentle or high rising waves,
days you host heron, minnows, sandpipers and gulls,
all your nightly offerings outside our summer window:
loon calls from dark distances or near coves.

Now, with summer's end I must step away. Good bye.

But through the miles I will dream your water
as it turns toward ice, your first freeze, shifts and creaks
in pounding cold. Around your shores
survival will show in the tall pines.

Inside our own shuttered place, pots and dishes, rugs
and blankets, all things temporarily not needed,
will freeze and thaw, freeze and thaw
while you stay solid as the deep season lingers.

By winter's end who knows how soon
your ice will first melt and on what edges,
when your deeply frozen mass will crack
and when wind will force your ice to form tall walls
that heave and collapse along the shores.

In spring we will be back
for surprises we never foresee.

Gone

Say it gently.
Whisper to the wind.
My husband is dead.

Questions only he could answer
flutter winter south. Names of species
taken with him   gone.

Gone   diagnoses   word derivations
sudden sightings   eagle   owl   unfound
when he’s no longer by my side.

Gone all books we planned to read aloud.
No new personas can now come alive.
I will simply read to underline.

Accounts he would savor
no longer to share.
Silent birds in an empty land.

Ode to Not Knowing

After the accident
after the call
my brother
driving me to the hospital
the emergency room
a woman by my side
Would you like . . . Can I help . . .?
Can I get you . . .? I'm the chaplain . . .."

No. Nothing.
I am looking for my husband.
He was simply swimming in the pool.
He'll be sitting in a chair
dazed by water   waiting for his name
maybe on a gurney
or temporary bed.

Asleep. He's asleep.
Dave? David?
I don't dare kiss his lips
for here
he belongs to someone else.
So many hushed words
my quick query   *Is he all right?*
No need to ask. He has to be.
I'll speak for myself. I'll tell myself,
they're taking him   somewhere else.

Upstairs in some room or hall
the chaplain   sudden sister   lets me talk.

I want to go on   go on
tell about Dave   tell about family
tell her   tell her   all I can do   is tell
my words spill
like the water must have poured from his mouth
swimming   just swimming   in the pool.
I hear   *He's down the hall.*
An hour passed   an hour gone?

Someone will be phoning   to the kids   to grand-kids
my hands hold my stomach tight
my innards want   who's to hold me?

I'm sure that   soon
I'll be in that room   with him again
back with you   Dave
and everything will be okay.
I'll thank God.
Just as long as you are all right.

Fallen from History

By parachute, great white silken cloud,
I dropped down hard
on unfamiliar ground
from one high window of the hospital's ICU.
Tangled in bunting soft-as-skin,
our shared history stopped
with a jolt.
Your body, left behind.

Some few hours earlier
you'd tossed your swimming gear
on the car's back seat. Our final words
can never grow sufficient.
You, leaving for your drowning.

We've spent storms together.
I never believed you would let go,
drawn into the eye that follows sailors
on faint days with its steel shadow.
You, master of control,
you, ready to console any distressee.
Why not me?

I long to hold you in a last long hug
to stretch our history
stopped in that high room.
Would that an angel could fly me back
where you no longer lie, in the bed of goodbyes
you never heard.

In Search of You

Awake or half asleep I search for you,
even calling back your coma breath,
hours unsteadied before your sudden death.

I stare in windows near and far,
in mirrors that may still hold you,
I cannot let you disappear.

My fingers ride your handwriting
on notes you scribbled to me yesterday.
I'll hoard samples of your signature, my surname.

Typing papers needed for your death
I feel the braille of you on every key,
every word you tapped imprinted on my inner life.

I see you skimming with lingering birds
that winter-weave through black tree limbs,
you show as shining gems of ice below my tracks.

Without you I proceed without a clue
through winter to upcoming spring,
all newly unfamiliar seasons
primed to animate a new life.

Rescues

One year a Boston hurricane
broke our landline to the world.
We took off, you and I, driving north
past felled trees,
following the disaster swath.

In the dark depths of our get-away
you laid a fire, starting the blaze.
From another room I called, *Is the damper open?*

No! You found the metal bucket,
pulled out the straggled twigs,
branches, newspaper, already afire,
tumbled with the bucket of flames
though the unlit room,
out the door, over the porch,
and onto the beach.
Just in time you dumped
the blazing array into the lake.
You were, as always,
glad to save us from disaster.

Yet last night my dreaming mind broke down my old car.
I was far from home, acting on your directions
to get an estimate, drifting
from garage to soiled and oily cashier's office.

Six thousand five hundred, not the fifty in cash
I held ready in my pocket. When you came for me,
you could not change their money-minds
any more than I could, nor did you try—
you decided I could handle the car, left me
to drive that crazy rocking-horse home alone.

Invisible

Lights out. Clocks stopped.
I would reach for you   my love
If you were here
          but alone
in darkness I fumble
chair to chair   chair to
table
looking for the always that is not you
but should be.
How smooth the table's top   comforting
lamp-post cool and slim
how strong I am at grabbing.

Door knob   door jam.
Kitchen's cold dark water.
I drink the dark delicious   my insides
chilled.
I feel the counter
place
my invisible glass.

The nothing that exists
removes all I would rush to salvage
notebooks   poems   papers
dark unseen laptop lost in nowhere
          and you.

In this blackout
our soft couch receives me.
No   I won't try each switch.
When light returns
with its fine vigor
what will still be here?

Only the Sea Beside Me

Snails move
as I move,
slow as a sigh.

Like those tight clingers,
seeming low in spirit, nondescript,
I too would cling to damp
but sun-warmed satin rocks
or creep, barely noticed,
toward alternate anchorage—
some high deserted tide pool.

Alone,
I must moor
where no one will notice,
ashamed of my re-size,
like some failed child
assigned a new and lower level.

I cannot loosen—needing
to stay in practice as my solo self.
Forgive me, dear friends
for my attachment to these stones,
this distant shore,
my pullback condition, for now,
too powerful to contradict.

If touched, my invisible footing
hastily retreats, by instinct—
my whole being flicks shut,
my interior, sealed.

Why I Can't Go Out

I dare not go out. Leave you alone?
Spirits, like toddlers, need innovative watchers.
Who knows? You might tumble down-stairs
and break a neck.
Oh, I forget, you no longer need a neck.

You might try to reset clocks
as you once did each daylight savings.
Loose springs hung out and dangling
would leave us both time-less.

And what of telephones?
Trial dialing could bring questions
harder than *Number please?*
If you cannot speak to your wife,
how then to a robot?

A spirit may walk easily through walls
leaving no silhouette-shaped holes
for a wife to patch. But
how fearsome for you, dear lost one,
searching every room
to find me absent. I cannot allow
new trauma.

Should curiosity set you rummaging,
you might test the burners
hoping to re-enact our morning rituals.
From a distance I might hear
firetrucks out front, loud speakers,
men hosing flames or suiting up to go in.
Too dangerous. Nothing even to consider.
My presence at home, clearly essential.

Nightland

I wouldn't do it,
wouldn't dare, don't know
what to do by day.
But when at night
the catnapped brain meanders
to another land,
time to light a match.

I've stacked
the starter-kindling of the past,
collected willfully—
rubbish of complaints, questions ignored,
sheer detritus of demands.
Dump it in, all. Light it.

By the fire little sunfish,
you're barely edible. Much knife-work needed.
Be careful. I'm still here.
Only if I'm awake
is anyone safe.

Downsizing

down
down
to the half place
ready to meet you there
as if I am ready
I am not ready
I just need to say
at least
I remember

let me keep what you lived for
or not keep
at least first love letters, wedding pictures
who can decide the value
of all that passed since we first met
or came after you knocked on my door

at least I remember
no birds fly
in dim space
nor do crickets likely chirp
where the half-made
half-done half-gone
done and gone
live with those objects of memory
silent-of-song

at least I remember
at our summer retreat
arriving in spring

you letting our dog from the car
to bark and circle with freedom and delight
wine on the porch
listening to the jungle peepers of spring
released that evening for us alone
each year my believing I had never heard
sounds of this jungle night
before

at least I remember
so I must go
down
down
to meet you
half under
only in our lower level after all
where family members always stay on visits
call it a walk-out apartment
as once we did

come back to see
for I am surely downsizing you and me
this lot in file cabinets
containers and shelves
at least
your work here is done

Dazed October

Outside the bright glass
in my new resized rooms,
red spooks drift and turn.
One oak leaf nearby quivers,
horizontals out of sight.
Tired leaf, tired body, wincing eyes
that last night said *just*
sleep.
Let slightness slip
here in this first apartment, my own.

Long ago, before the cliff of marriage,
last apartment living—
Quaker meetings
near my shared flat on Beacon Hill.
Sunday mornings in the patio.
The deep smell of earth,
walls rising around our silence.
Down drifted
the voices of children.

Here, in the gully below my window,
leaf-covered branch-covered twigs settle.
Autumn plants collapse against the slope
across the way.
No voices.
Just telephone's singsong.

Mine?
No.
Wind chimes rise from what I only know
as below.

The Nightmare Theatre

What is ignited by dream will not burn
what any bad thought may crave to obliterate.

The magic sparrow rises from the night forest
and with sparkling songs lights secret hiding places
to spark tonight's nightmare theater—I search
deserted houses for missing cards to finish the game
no one will ever play by day. Oh, the poison. The curtain
closes. *Don't leave me alone. What game will no one play?*
Why won't you play? What poison? Thank God, awake.

The theater opens, another night's production.
On lone streets I run with revelers carrying high
stalactites made from my held-back tears.
I will not cry. I will not cry or will I cry?
Why not show my tears to those I know so well?

I climb to the edge and throw the match that lights
the sunset fire. Lightening flares. Let the damn world burn!
No. The controlled burn to stop all fires. Let all fires cease.

Caught in Dreams

Night, let me be a passive traveler in your dark woods.
I live in deep down replays every day. No need
to plunge me through all of London to find my alarm.
Hold back your teasing metaphors—I am not a crow.

No more crumb-path clues leading to an empty page.
No hurricane instructions for a past calamity.
The once-best friend hidden in a husband's name—
stop the search. No lost bundle of Irish cash or lost address.

Give me no bear prince to entertain as royalty,
no great great aunt begging to move in.
My brilliant ponderings finally released in print—
the book banned. No. And No to more flunked exams.

Lay me down for sleep. Through each upcoming scene
please place my character in more gentle distress.

Not to Say Goodbye

He still lives with me.
When I visit you, he'll come too.

Please don't be alarmed.
We've all been good friends.

Just don't ignore him. Act familiar.
As always, use his name.

Reminisce, speak freely even if you know
a spirit can not reply. Should certain memories

cause me to rear back like a pony
rattled by a snake—don't worry. Remember,

I survived the memorial. Catastrophe
has passed. For me, nothing less

disturbs a day. If you should offer
a bowl of fresh fruit, please divide in two

any orange, peach, or apple, even grapes,
half for me and half for my dear other.

Fare Well

Dear leaf, you float downstream
on the slowly moving surface,
your recent brilliance gone, passing
with the fading glory of Autumn.

I walk along the bank to watch
your final course, you, once stable
now detached from your source
discolored as discarded paper.

You swirl as in procession, caught
with the fallen—pine-needle clumps,
maple wings, generations of twigs,
all too recently transformed.

As if in ritual transit, the gentle current
sends your remains to ride alone, gliding
over pale slanted grass, ripped moss,
waterlogged trunks the beavers felled.

A sudden pull and your bearer, the stream,
lets you go. Lost in the lake's expanse,
moved only by the dip and churl of water,
you disappear into daydreams and memory.

Fair winds and gentle waves.

THREE

Ghazal for You Who Left

The hurt the hurt the pain. Unchain me from what's left,
this life, what's left. What's left?

Once one plus one meant two. To one anew we grew,
our sides together fixed. Now one without. What's left?

You were my home, at home. Or far away we phoned each day.
No more. Homeless within my home. What's left?

Must I carry you? Inside, like one more baby, too late, and you,
no baby you? Where will you remain? What's left?

The story of the stream, how small waves, caught by stones,
find new routes. Otherwise, what's left? What else is left?

In the garden of my mind I'll fly, I'll fly on sun-filled days,
to find my shadow's artistry. If not, what's left?

New sprouts point rocket tips, soon lilies of the valley.
For solace even the moon might do. What's left?

The world is left. And left to know its sights and swirls, I too
must grow. Must Libby grow? I guess. How else to see what's left?

Fast Fading

You are not alive tonight, anywhere I try to place you.
Am I alive or somewhere else?
With your sharp knife you travel zone to zone
cutting scenes that once existed, while
I travel in place, locked in the puzzle of finding you.
In my single zone, outside the window
your favorite birds assemble, sometimes sudden
as flickering shadows. I sense darkness.
Not you, dear one? I dare not glance.
Were you really mine, the You in photographs?
Let me come alive before I fail to trust in us.
And everything around me fades to shadow.

I strain to keep you safe in Technicolor.
Memories flick like birds behind my eyes.

Awakening Villanelle

Stay away, stay away night.
Morning comes with a hint of today
halting the chase, leaving the dead to their dwellings.

Sleep, strenuous sleep. Take away streamers of dreams,
lingering riddles. Dawn alights desire for courage.
Stay away. Stay away, night.

Balms of today—soothing wind, turnover waves
dispel all sights that harshly lived as harshly moved,
halt the chase, leaving the dead to their dwellings.

Let morning prickle skin, reach bone and sinew.
Let demands become mere shadows flattened.
Night, stay away, stay away.

Expel me from the realm of make believe.
I'm ready. Bring forth this day.
Cease the chase, leave the dead to their dwellings.

Released at last, recalled to sacred life,
the sleeper will arise again.
Stay away, stay away, night.
Halt the chase, leave the dead in far distance.

Snow Garden

Because it snowed last night, south in Somerville,
do not speak of almost-April, or spring. Tulips tinted
with pale striations are no tulips, but soon-to-be stricken
memories of hopes and distress from this past winter.

Because I doubt our strivings strong enough
to hold us safely in this season's altered time,
let me not extol lavish branches glowing in morning white.
What matter if they carry lush magical light?

False flamingos bending to sip snow, giant
snow-frogs, once this garden's anchoring boulders
and a pathetic snow-bear hunched behind the fullest
flowerings, peach, purple, lemon would-bes of delight.

I ask again—how to restrain this once-welcome rebirth,
returning in overheated force, too soon.

Blank Page

In the lamp-lit room
with wooden floor   wooden walls
picture gallery
of well-stained boards
blank paper and ready pen

I sit
while humming creatures slip through
blinking my light with their bodies
brushing my bare places

outside   moonlit minnows glide
beside the dock
frogs
patrol dark avenues of swamp light
and from small deserted beaches
they speak   pause   speak
yes   oh yes   oh yes

if my spirit will not ride the dark
on columns of light
move time to space
here into there
if words don't come as a flood of stars

I will wait
in the dim room, amid small wild fragile things
the moving of multiple wings
their barely audible plunging
until

no longer waiting
the mind can fish in water or air
loving what it loves   catching its finds
making what it makes
on this or the other side
of night

Front and Back, Dark and Light

> *Now I am going to sit down in this chair, facing you.*
> *Draw me as if you were seeing me from behind.*
> —Tancred Saraceni to artist Francis Cornish,
> from Robertson Davies, *What's Bred in the Bone*

I see you, my back, nape of my neck, shoulder blades,
back of my life with the eyes of my mind. But when I raise
the ivory mirror, expecting its reflection to work illusions,
the back world of my own mind's making disappears—

leaving only a roomful of familiar space, held in a moment
of invisible time. I flash the mirror to the sun. It sends
back a flight of golden birds. I appraise the undersides
of my arms—fresh as new life, the softness of baby skin.

The undersides of my feet, rough worn pads, recall
a lifetime of tracks. On the reverse of my hand,
on my bright palm encoded, lie the paths that could be
lines to the opposite side of the world,
evening lamps lit in China while in Vermont, bright dawn
brings a sky-full of snow to revise our lives.

Footprints

Above my head, footprints
        on the ceiling.
Footprints,
        an upside-down path
into time.
Footprints that for years
have never faded,
never walked away.

        Not everyone can say
that once a stranger
walked on their ceiling boards,
lifted them high, then
said good bye.

        Before sleep,
on my ceiling I take a walk.
Have you seen the hoof print
on my cheek, above my left eye?
In another age
avid villagers might have seen me
on the street, suspicious—
Someone trod on her bedroom ceiling!
I heard a face-marked poet is a witch.

I try to live like everyone else
but sometimes I do seek Elsewhere—

deep down underground in caves
where footprints also walk as petroglyphs
and hands of mine sketch from the past
scenes on marked walls.

If tonight in dream time
I'm cast out of town, I'll find a wild woods,
careful to step free of fragile moss,
leaving no footprints, only words
scratched on scattered birchbark.

I'll find treats—
chestnuts, walnuts, acorns,
sweet and bitter raspberries,
thimbleberry juice marking my hand,
daisies, buttercups, everywhere
the scent of fresh-fallen boughs.

Soft stones I will stroke,
their flat or pocked marks
once made and remade
by this earth
before we knew of time.

Finally Rain

finally rain   to swirl   ricochet
on-the-way rain
this lake too low   no rain
until today   when mountain tears
soak drought's dry sand
and dulled strewn pebbles

rain   pummels first
a whole tribe of fish
up to note what's new   their circles interspersing
on the lake's churned surface

pine branches   tall against white sky
shiver at the touch
of heavy drops   flitting off dry needles
remnant rain
slips through to find the fern-floor

wide-spread clouds of spray   in the meadow
shake like sails in wind
rain
where asters   goldenrod
barely flower within tall grasses
high and low rain   skimming   flying
pounding rain

rain falls on ants' homes   the old tree
that long-ago lightning struck down
rain   soaks the thick load
of lichens   mushrooms   brittle mosses

rain finds the almost-empty stream bed
rain   rain   fills a dip   a deep and barren trough
minute pools
trickle to start a down-flow

the mouth of earth opens

After Rain

Willow leaves
still green
in Autumn's super light
press long pale undersides
against my windowpane.
Startled by wind,
they flee up the glassy wall,
stems rattling, racing,
before they slip.
Heavy drops,
clear bloated beads
alight, creep, freeze
into a spider-inspired
transparency.

Ethereal replicas.
Leaf shapes, cloud webs,
floating
in an ice-colored
cobbled sky.

Will I ever be ready?

To the Sleeping Artist

After Francisco Goya's etching,
The Sleep of Reason Produces Monsters

Artist, you slump
while darkness fills around you.
Relief is but an empty bowl; sleep,
abyss to absence.

In the nightfall of sky, monsters,
sharp-beaked, jagged-winged, fly to find you.
Beware. Even your cat, suddenly feral,
lynx-faced, joins them.

Exhausted, yes. But have you abandoned
your brush, your pen, leaving empty pages
when you, with the deftness of your art
could lead us toward reason?

You sleep though demonic eyes peer
over your great-coat, winged creatures
find your feet; owl-eyed bats crowd
to reach your limp body.

How can you ignore such treacherous commotion,
mobs following carriers of falsehoods
and fake hopes, set loose,
looking for those to hate, to blame?

Brush off the swarms rabid with enmity,
before their wings lodge in your uncovered hair.
Monsters multiply, incitements heavy on their wings.
We need you. Open your eyes.

The City and the Sea

The city breaks in houses to the sea . . .
—Charles Reznikoff

the sea   moves toward the city
slowly wanting the city
which has no place to go
for the sea
having no place to go
needs
            space
from the city
        streets that cross avenues
avenues that cross streets
            surfaces unready
for the slick shine of salt water

waiting
taxis   walkers   sight-seers   theater-goers
            signs
saying Lincoln Center
or warning of change
billboards speak in colors
the earth or sun do not share

fast-passing people
push toward stairways marked *this way to the subway*
        where   down below

some one or two or more may one day
step in the sea

        on the way to work   to home
to watch WNET news
      or turn off the news
saying *the news is getting too much for me*
a pause too slight to see
and the city
          moves
toward the sea

Whale Songs

We need you, deep divers.
Your songs roll through the underwater world.
Here we are, or, *We're on our way,*
back-boomings arrive as you arch the deep.
Yes, I too have listened for the rolling currents
that consummate the songs of life.

Water bathes your bodies in great basins.
Your sounds, below the swells, travel further
than phrases sung by our sopranos:
heartbreaking conundrums rising in the sanctuary.

Long ago we slid out of oceans, trying balloons
of sound in air, in wind. You slipped back.
Now you carry fluid memory for us,
underwater ballads the ballast of our longing
to touch our past, to touch you, to consecrate
the vocabulary of landed language.

Kindling

Kindling, my job, my joy. Even old leaves' fermenting scents,
connotations of rottage, sink with delight into my avid senses.
I cannot overlook one tight decrepit tree knot or pine offering.
Eager I am to handle, to stroke each beat-up remnant,
last night's storm-surged bits, thrashed into this cove and caught,
each fire starter with its story of breakage, of calamity,
having served as witness—dog-chewed branch or gnarled ball,
baby-rocked all winter in lake's deepest cold cradle,
wild root segment, mother-grasping its round smooth stone,
proud feather, standing tall on its spent-log pedestal,
light-as-bone driftwood cut into twelfth-lengths,
plus two lines of rope in rusty decay, rife for rhyming.

I will stay among lakeside treasures. What more desired?
Grateful for splinters and unraveled ends to start my fires.

Shadow Play

In the slant fire of orange sky,
fields glow with inner green
and I follow you, long shadow,
stretched ahead like upcoming thoughts.

Today tree shadows too
seem the thoughts of trees
as I crisscross open fields,
the laid-out end of day.

My shadow, you lead me
strolling the pathways of my life,
but you cannot remain my guide.
You are but shade, come with light.

You hold no portents,
we will not merge, even at noon.
Unlike me, you overlay your past.
Of your future, no hint.

I'll twirl my arms
to make a bird of you!
I'll lead you through high grass, purple asters,
glowing stones. Catch *them* if you can.

But it's getting late,
and darkness will get you first.

Children of Midnight

Silent lake   night still warm.
Midnight. Out in dusky fog
  alone.

In the wild cove nearby
the uptick of water   oars splashing? Swimmers?
Too still for waves. No one nearby.
Who's out? Who's there? No answer.

Through overgrown reeds
and washed-in leaves
a boat full of children drifts in.

    Are they—?   Could they be
    our children   yours and mine? Our three
        but younger?   It cannot be. So many.
    Yes. They're ours   our children at every age
    as they were—
        then and then and then   toddlers and ten-year-olds

    little and big   dozens. How well I know
    that plump little arm   the careful hand steadying
    a gunnel   a little body bailing,
    a profiled face just changed by puberty.
    I know all—sundry excitements
    the face raised to starlight   the long-tangled hair.
        By time so long ago dispersed.

I want to pull in their boat. But I'm slow.
The craft scrapes bottom. Children race
beyond the beach   under the first trees
almost to the little woods. They scramble with flashlights
creating each other from darkness.
Fireflies flash too   in and out of tall grass.

The littlest hide   fitting themselves behind trees.
Others run—searching for old havens?
Who's it? Who's it?
Fast moving beams scribble up and down trees.

By the water some children dig
with quick children's hands   the rusting spade.
Sand flies up. Digging or building as they used to
until they too are running.

Finally   my feet let me race after them.
How gently I call
how gently they disappear.

Huckleberries

I have to hurry, or I'll never find her.
Mom looks past her newspaper.
You can finish your breakfast.
She'll be around. There's no rush.

I sit back down, chew and swallow.
Am I free now? I reach for the old beach pail
stained huckleberry blue.
Take some coins from the pot.
Don't go far.

Huckleberries?
Where is the ghost who lives in that voice?
Town people say, *Be careful of the Huckleberry Woman.*
No one lets people like her inside.
They say she'd steal an apple off your kitchen table.
She takes off, fast as she comes
and the bulges in her pockets are wings.

Huckleberries?
She comes from high-up far
where wild people burn the tops of hills
to make more berries grow.
Her kind are richer than we know.
Coins jingle in their hankies.
And that's not all.
Strangers like the Huckleberry Woman
grab empty land—that's where they live.

Huckleberries?
She's crossing at the light,
so quick you'd think she's running
to sell berries to the fire hydrant.

Huckleberries?
I run so fast
my mind can find the high burned places
where her wild children
play with foxes and wolves.

They stay up all night
and follow the moon with their bright eyes.
Before we're up they're swimming in the wind.
They leap where new sprouts
pop through the black burn.
Those kids really are rich with berries,
berries to throw, berries to turn each other blue
wrestling with their huckleberry-blue hands.
They can squish berries under their bare toes,
blue children who smell like the pail in my hand.

Huckleberry Woman! I've caught up and she hears.
She kneels, brings down her big tub in front of me.

Do you steal children? I whisper.
She pours blue into my pail,
berries bumble over the sides, onto the sidewalk.

She takes the coins from my hand,
under my finger hooks the handle of my pail.
Up goes her tub of huckleberries
to rest again on its high stand.
She rises, she flies.

Come Back and Be My Loon

If you were a loon, you could spend
all spring, all summer at this lake,
paddling our well-loved water ways.
You would fish, dip and dive
through shallow and deep currents
in the secret zones below.
All season, my love, nearby.

Glide past the dock for me to swim alongside.
Glimpse the rest of your lost kin on shore,
shaded beneath pine boughs,
chatting, reading, or raking sand
to keep the raw beach smooth.

Moon-lit nights, I would sit by my window
waiting to see you on the lake,
your long calls echoing from stream to cove to inlet.
Soul to soul, your spectral notes
soothing my sleep

until late August
when ocean messages reach
your memory-need for flight to loon-winter,
away from this frozen lake.

I would watch your shaky practice take-offs,
your antique bird-self barely equipped for flight.
You would rise and leave.
On shore I'd stand,

staring at the sky above the mountains,
sorrowing for your long Atlantic winter,
bobbing in salt waves.

In spring though, you'd be back.
I'd be ready then to wish you a new partner,
beautiful in the loon way.

Day Lilies

Good bye,
Yesterday.
I snip off sorrow for
the loss of our shared day.
Yesterday, my balm,
you came as spring,
the last
of eight beauties.
Oh, to stop
the too-fast
tumbling
of your swift life.

I hold you, Yesterday,
wrinkled, shriveling,
reshaped
in my hand, a small pile
of soft skins.

But in the morning
a fresh delight
out near the old wood pile—
wide-petaled, extravagant,
strong-stemmed,
the lasting spirit
of yellow life, blooming
Today.

Entreaty

Time, set me free
to find the rarest imprint stamped
within a dried-out leaf,
shadows
that mark the sun-filled meadow before dusk,
pathways that gleam within a spider's web,
and the bright shivers
that remain
to spark fresh light
above the stream's bed.
For now,
I will not say
the bear's good-night.
Lead me gently
through this season
where we can see-saw,
child-like with bright display,
beside the hidden edge
of winter.

Thank You

Your notes lift me from my everydays,
your whispers save me from wolf-ways.
Each sound soothes my soul, even in darkness.
Poetry, you replace my burned-out lights.
I've learned new habits searching for your turns.
Ring the bell, I'm right beside you at the table.
I've sipped from glasses filled by tries,
you refill each empty glass with brand new tastes.
When you've been missing, I listen at the door.
Disturb me please, relieve my heavy mind.
Sometimes it's easier speaking to a page—
I'm ready here to greet you, pen in hand.

No need for sleep if you conduct my night.
Now or never, Poetry, any time.

About the Author

Vermont poet Libby VanBuskirk has published poems in *The Beloit Poetry Journal, The Orchards Poetry Journal, Quartet, Passager,* and other journals and anthologies. She published a book of short stories, *Beyond the Stones of Machu Picchu.*

She won the Barbara Carlin grant-award from The Society of Children's Book Writers for a picture book story, a national award from *Mademoiselle Magazine* which culminated in an interview with T.S. Eliot, and a poetry prize from *Writers' Digest.* She has also been nominated for Best of the Net.

After graduating from Wheaton College, VanBuskirk studied writing at Radcliffe Institute, University of Vermont, and through poetry seminars with Vermont poets David Weinstock and Rebecca Starks. She will forever miss her psychiatrist husband who died suddenly, but she has pushed on to create a new life.

For more about Libby VanBuskirk, see her website:
Libbypoetry.com

www.ingramcontent.com/pod-product-compliance
Lightning Source LLC
LaVergne TN
LVHW010627100826
845148LV00014B/3136
9798901466018